GOODNIGHT VOLUSIA

by Dr. Tyler Schmitz

No part of this publication may be reproduced in whole or in part, or stored in a retrieval system, or transmitted in any form or by any means, electronic, mechanical, photocopying, recording, or otherwise, without written permission of the author, except for the inclusion of brief quotations in a review. For information regarding permission, please write to: info@BarringerPublishing.com.

Copyright © 2025 Dr. Tyler Schmitz. All rights reserved.

Barringer Publishing, Naples, Florida • www.BarringerPublishing.com

ISBN: 978-1-954396-94-4

Library of Congress Cataloging-in-Publication Data
Goodnight Volusia / Dr. Tyler Schmitz

Printed in USA

To my twins, Luke and Landon—may you always discover magic in every moment and joy in every step. This book is for your endless curiosity and adventurous spirit.

Goodnight Volusia, where fun is in the air,
From sunny beaches to cool trails, adventure is everywhere!

Goodnight Blue Spring State Park, with waters so blue,
Watch manatees swim and play right in front of you!
You can splash in the spring or float in the sun,
Get ready for laughs and lots of fun!

Goodnight Daytona Beach, the World's Most Famous Beach,
Here there is so much fun all within reach!
From seeing motorcycles race to playing in the sand,
This wide sandy beach will make you a fan!

Goodnight Ponce Inlet Lighthouse, that stands up so high,
It looks over boats as they go by!
Climb to the top for a great view,
You'll see the ocean and skies so blue!

Goodnight Tomoka Park, a place rich with history,
Once the site of an ancient village, much of it a mystery!
Paddle, hike, or watch birds in the sky,
With trails waiting to be explored, discovery is standing by!

Goodnight Daytona Speedway, where engines roar as racers zoom by,
Cheer for your favorite car that goes by!
Here you can see race cars take flight,
Feeling the energy of speed is pure delight!

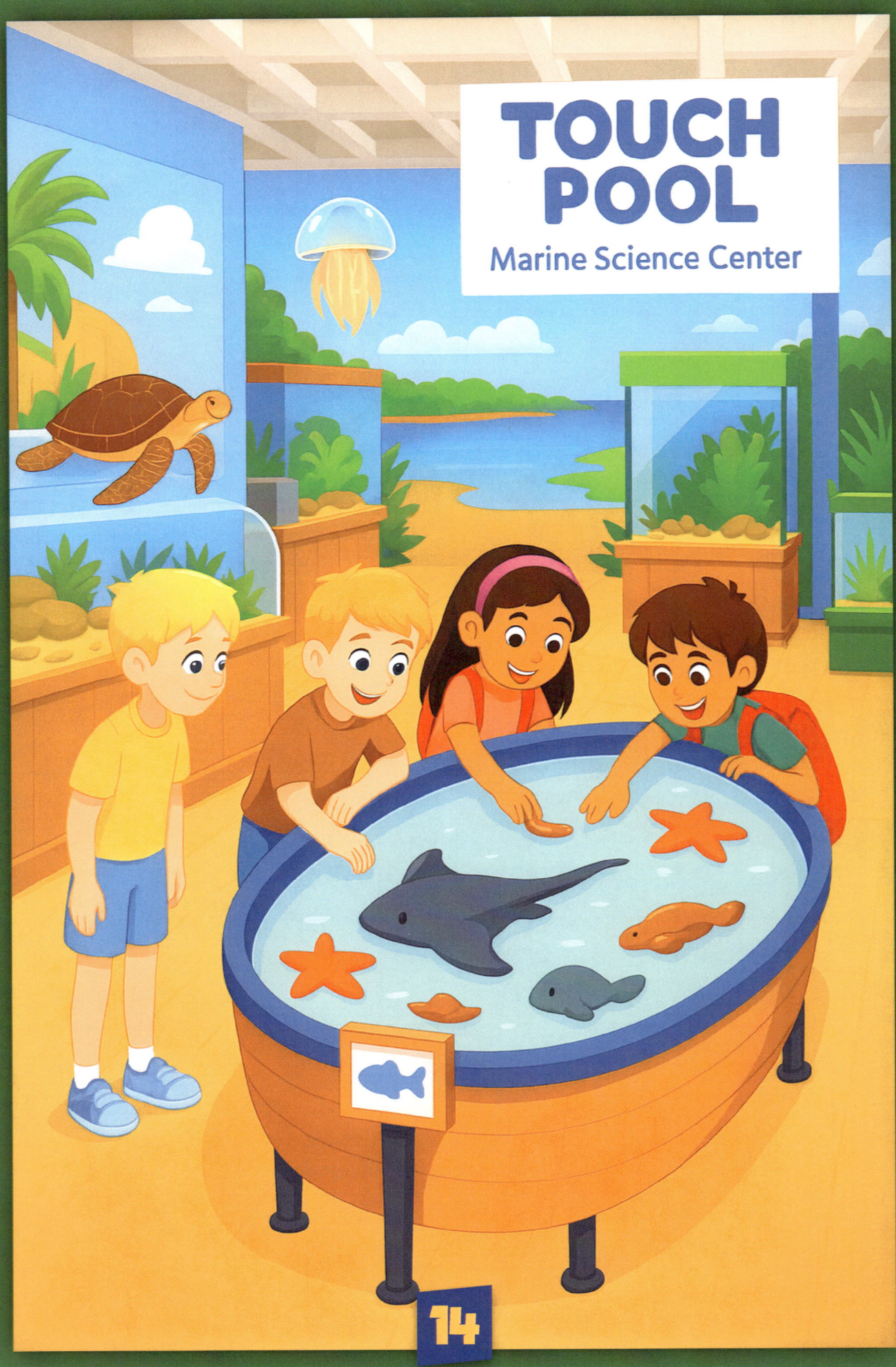

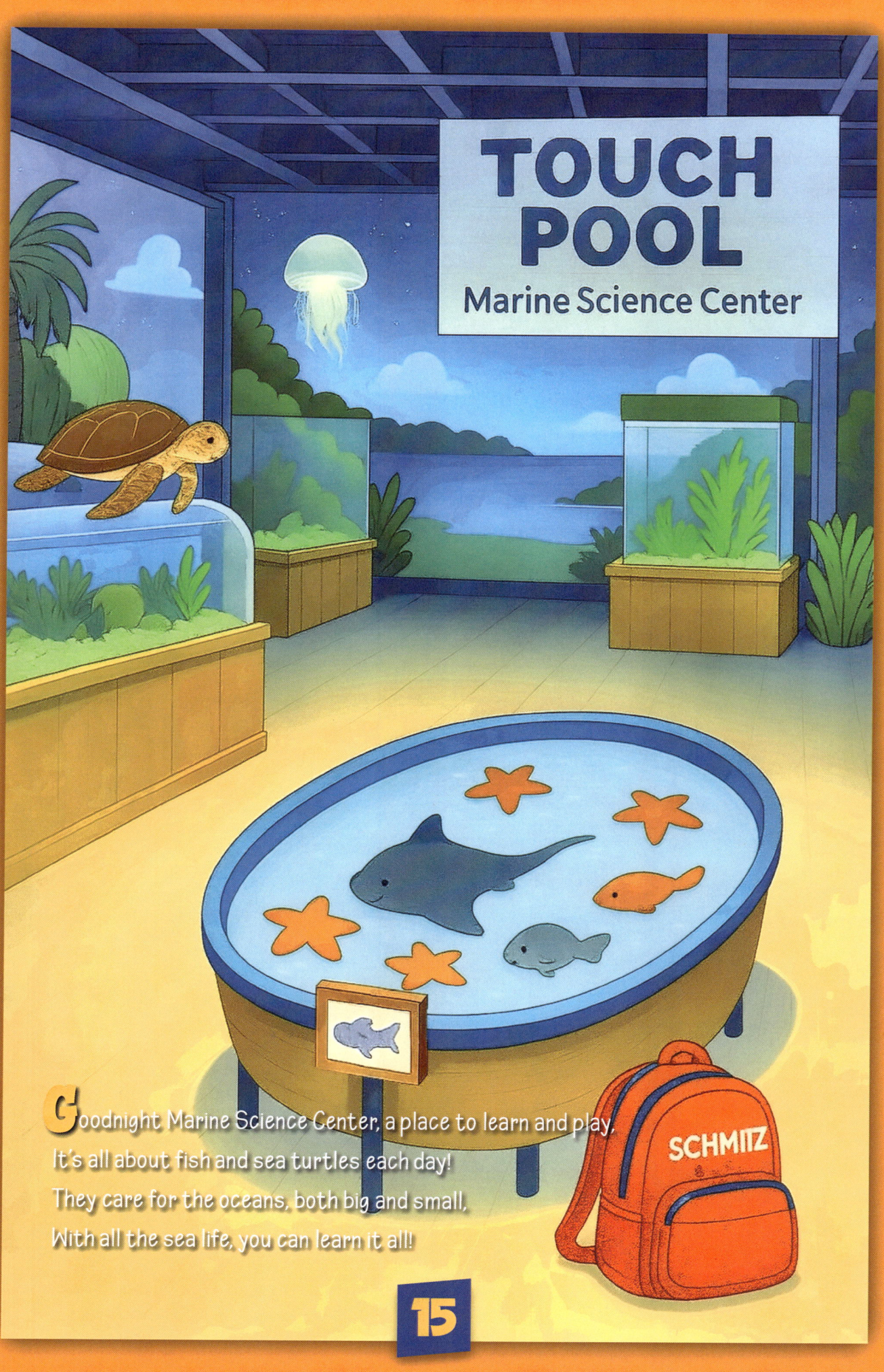

Goodnight Mosquito Lagoon, so calm, peaceful, and still,
You can fish or kayak and enjoy nature's thrill!
Watch seabirds flying high in the sky,
In this water, you can even see dolphins swimming by!

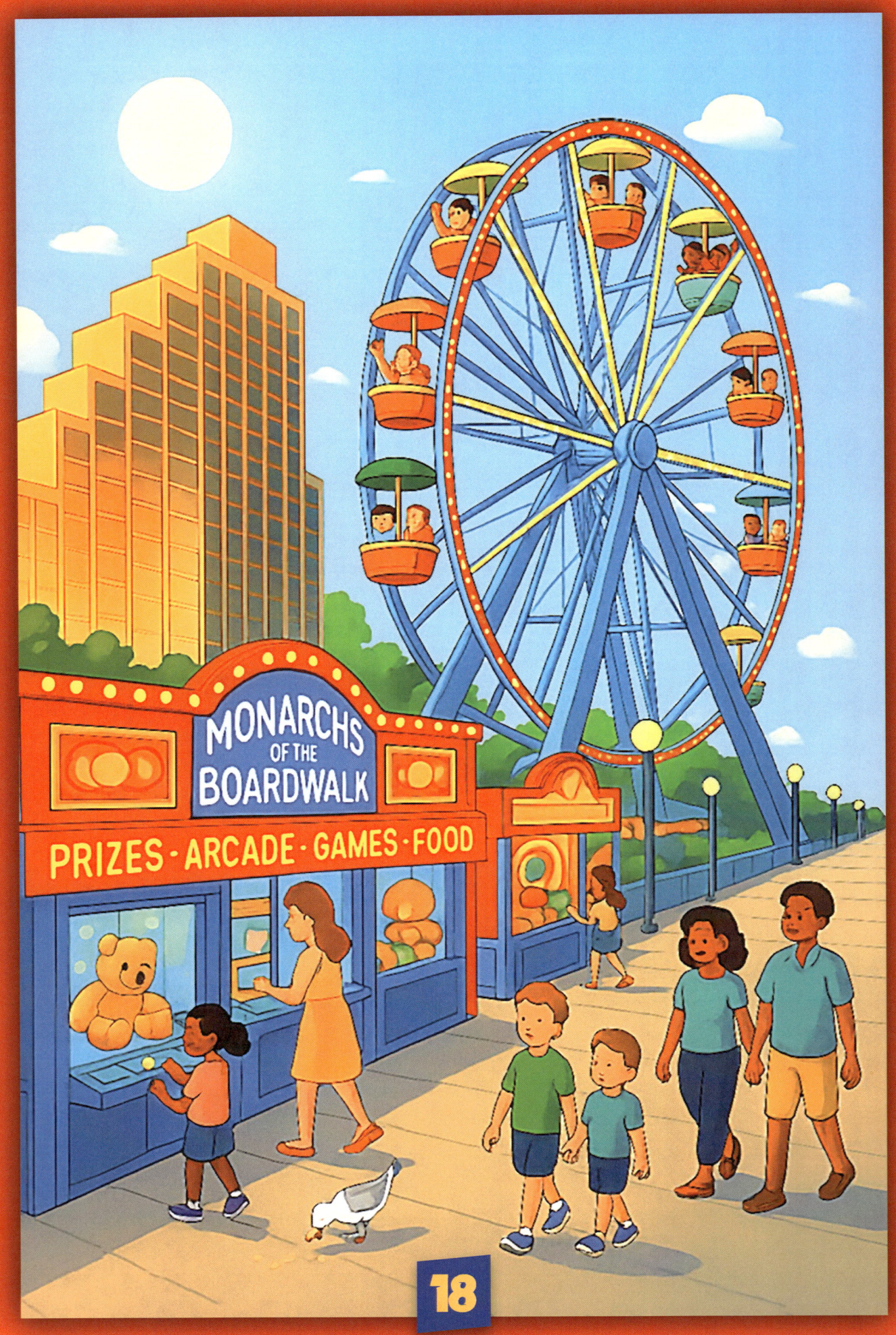

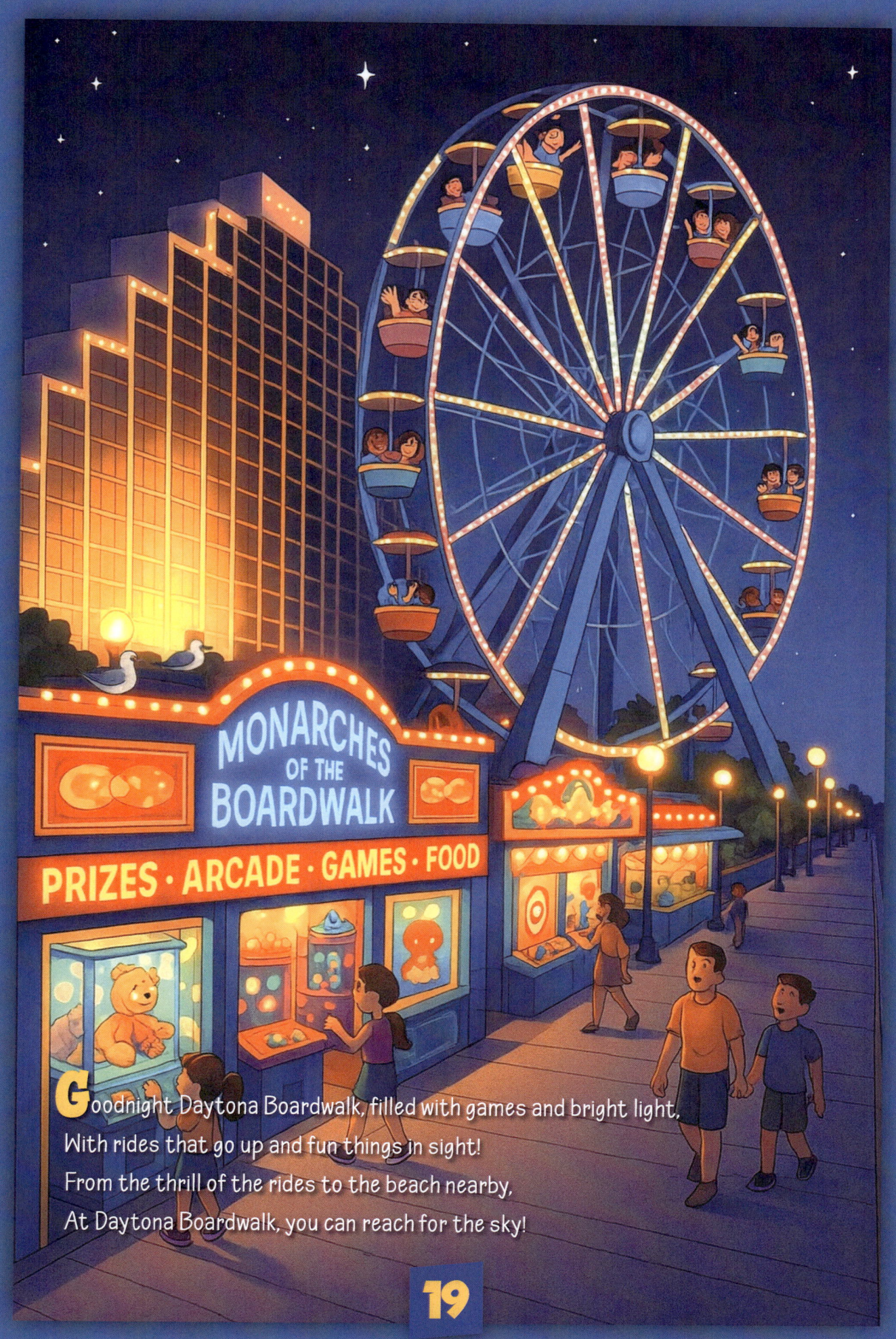

Goodnight Daytona Boardwalk, filled with games and bright light,
With rides that go up and fun things in sight!
From the thrill of the rides to the beach nearby,
At Daytona Boardwalk, you can reach for the sky!

Goodnight Green Springs State Park, where you can see alligators laying on logs,
Or walk through the live oaks to look for tree frogs!
This place is such a treasure to see,
With cool green waters and lots of green trees!

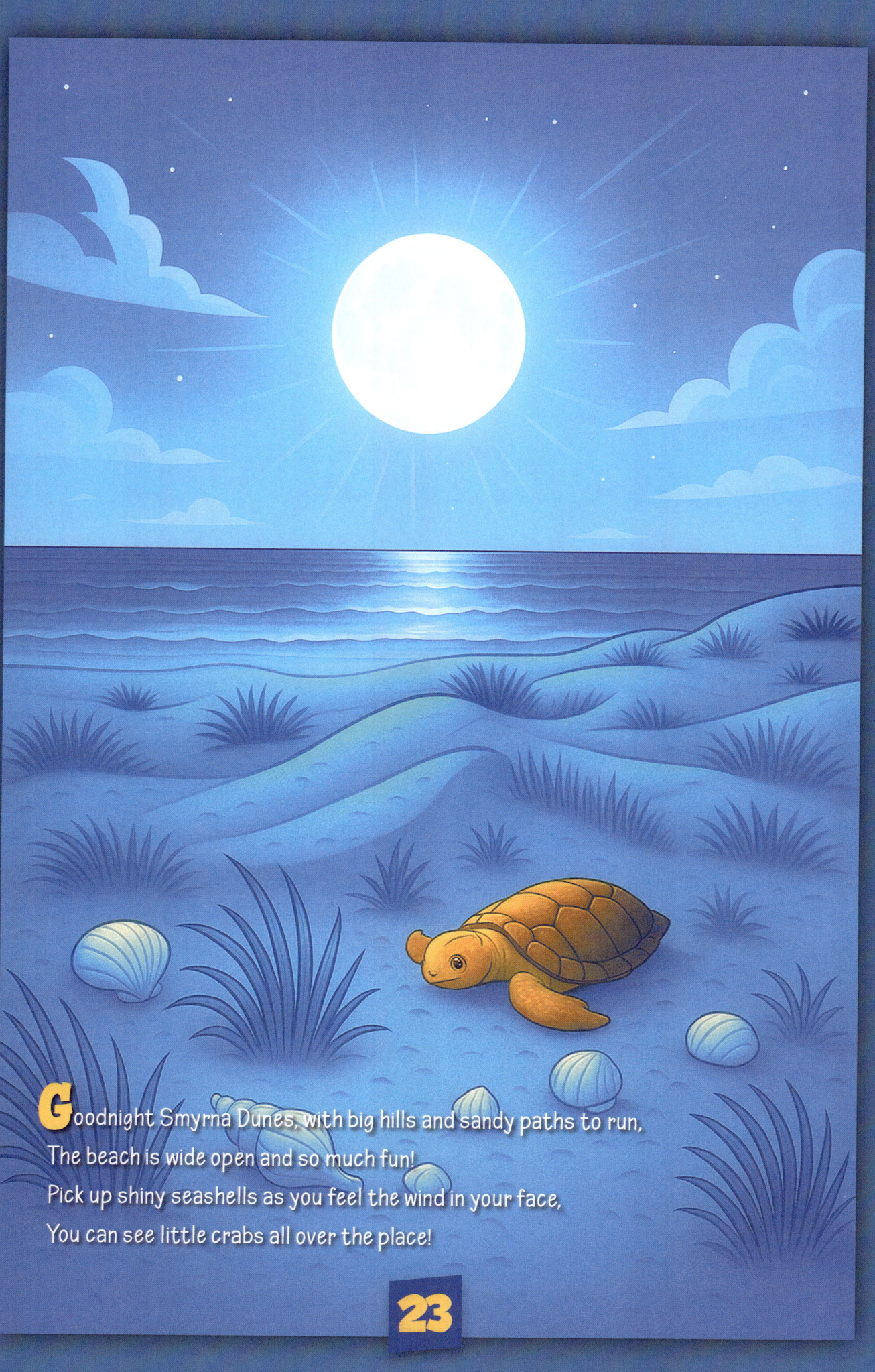

Goodnight Smyrna Dunes, with big hills and sandy paths to run,
The beach is wide open and so much fun!
Pick up shiny seashells as you feel the wind in your face,
You can see little crabs all over the place!

Goodnight Daytona Lagoon, where water is all around,
Slides go down fast, and fountains splash up from the ground!
You can float in the lazy river, feeling so free,
This water park is such a joy to see!

Goodnight New Smyrna Beach, where the surfers play,
Ride big waves and build sandcastles all day!
Ride your bicycle or walk on the land,
You can drive on the beach or feel the soft sand!

Goodnight East Central Rail Trail, the perfect place to bike,
Ride through the Florida scenery, it's a nature hike!
See all the wildlife and enjoy the fresh air,
On this 52-mile trail, you can ride anywhere!

Volusia County
FLORIDA

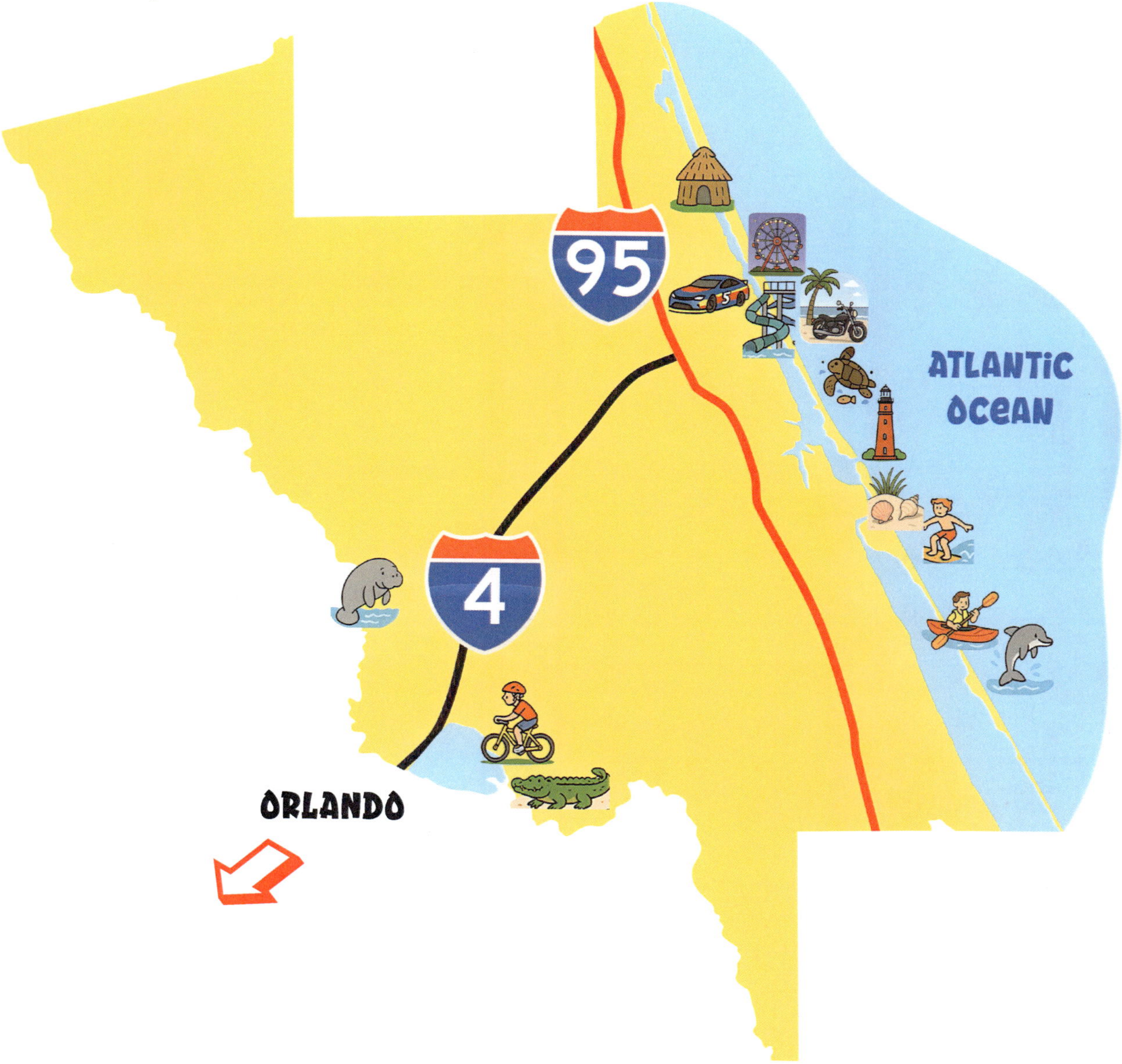

BLUE SPRING STATE PARK

A stunning natural oasis known for its crystal-clear spring waters, manatee viewing (especially in winter), swimming, kayaking, hiking trails, and picnicking amid lush scenery—ideal for families and nature lovers.

Address: 2100 W. French Ave., Orange City, FL 32763

More Info: Florida State Parks website (floridastateparks.org/parks-and-trails/blue-spring-state-park)

DAYTONA BEACH

World-famous for its 23 miles of wide, sandy shores perfect for driving on the beach, sunbathing, surfing, and events like Bike Week; it's a vibrant mix of relaxation and excitement.

Address: Main access at 1 S. Atlantic Ave., Daytona Beach, FL 32118 (visitor center)

More Info: Daytona Beach official tourism site (daytonabeach.com)

PONCE INLET LIGHTHOUSE

Florida's tallest lighthouse (175 feet) offers panoramic views from the top, maritime history exhibits, and a museum in a historic setting—climb for a workout and stunning ocean vistas.

Address: 4931 S. Peninsula Dr., Ponce Inlet, FL 32127

More Info: Ponce de Leon Inlet Lighthouse & Museum website (ponceinlet.org)

TOMOKA STATE PARK

A serene riverside park with ancient Native American history, fishing, canoeing, hiking trails through hammocks, and birdwatching—great for a peaceful outdoor escape.

Address: 2099 N. Beach St., Ormond Beach, FL 32174

More Info: Florida State Parks website (floridastateparks.org/parks-and-trails/tomoka-state-park)

DAYTONA INTERNATIONAL SPEEDWAY
Iconic NASCAR venue hosting the Daytona 500 and other races, with tours, a motorsports hall of fame, and high-speed experiences—thrilling for racing fans of all ages.

Address: 1801 W. International Speedway Blvd., Daytona Beach, FL 32114

More Info: Official Speedway website (daytonainternationalspeedway.com)

MARINE SCIENCE CENTER
An educational hub focused on marine life rehabilitation, with sea turtle hospital tours, touch tanks, bird exhibits, and interactive displays—perfect for kids and eco-enthusiasts.

Address: 100 Lighthouse Dr., Ponce Inlet, FL 32127

More Info: Marine Science Center website (marinesciencecenter.com)

MOSQUITO LAGOON
A pristine estuarine lagoon within the Canaveral National Seashore, renowned for fishing, kayaking, birdwatching, and bioluminescent paddling tours—part of Florida's "Indian River Lagoon" system.

Address: Access via Apollo Beach Visitor Center, 7611 S. Atlantic Ave., New Smyrna Beach, FL 32169

More Info: National Park Service website (nps.gov/cana/planyourvisit/mosquito-lagoon.htm)

DAYTONA BOARDWALK
A lively oceanfront promenade with amusement rides, arcades, shops, eateries, and the historic Bandshell for concerts—classic beachside fun and people-watching.

Address: 12 N. Ocean Ave., Daytona Beach, FL 32118

More Info: Daytona Beach Boardwalk website (daytonabeachboardwalk.com)

GREEN SPRINGS STATE PARK
A hidden gem with a vibrant green sulfur spring, picnic areas, walking paths, and historical significance—great for a relaxing, off-the-beaten-path visit.

Address: 994 Enterprise-Osteen Rd., Enterprise, FL 32725

More Info: Volusia County Parks website (volusia.org/services/community-services/parks-recreation-and-culture/parks-and-trails/park-facilities-and-locations/green-springs-park.stml)

SMYRNA DUNES PARK
A coastal dune ecosystem with boardwalk trails, beach access, fishing piers, and dog-friendly areas—excellent for hiking, wildlife spotting, and ocean views.

Address: 2995 N. Peninsula Ave., New Smyrna Beach, FL 32169

More Info: Volusia County Parks website (volusia.org/services/community-services/parks-recreation-and-culture/parks-and-trails/park-facilities-and-locations/smyrna-dunes-park.stml)

DAYTONA LAGOON WATER PARK
A family-friendly water park with slides, wave pools, lazy rivers, mini-golf, go-karts, and arcade games—splashy fun for beating the Florida heat.

Address: 601 Earl St., Daytona Beach, FL 32118

More Info: Official website (daytonalagoon.com)

NEW SMYRNA BEACH

A charming, artsy beach town with 17 miles of white-sand shores, surfing spots, galleries, dining, and the scenic Flagler Avenue—known for its laidback vibe and shark bite notoriety (but still safe and fun!). This beach is known as the "shark bite capital of the world".

Address: Visitor center at 223 Flagler Ave., New Smyrna Beach, FL 32169

More Info: New Smyrna Beach tourism site (visitnsbfl.com)

EAST CENTRAL REGIONAL RAIL TRAIL

A 52-mile multi-use trail (part of Florida's Coast-to-Coast Connector) for biking, walking, and horseback riding through scenic rural areas, wetlands, and towns—ideal for outdoor enthusiasts.

Address: Trailhead at Green Springs Park, 994 Enterprise-Osteen Rd., Enterprise, FL 32725 (one of several access points)

More Info: Florida Department of Environmental Protection website (floridadep.gov/parks/ogt/content/east-central-regional-rail-trail-state-trail)

"I hope you and your family get the chance to visit these wonderful places in Volusia and make memories of your own. Until then, may your dreams be filled with beaches, springs, trails, and sunshine—goodnight!"

—Tyler Schmitz

www.ingramcontent.com/pod-product-compliance
Lightning Source LLC
Chambersburg PA
CBRC092052040426
42451CB00005B/28